Imaginary Sonnets

Imaginary SONNETS

POEMS BY
Daniel Galef

WORD GALAXY PRESS
An imprint of Able Muse Press

Word Galaxy Press

www.wordgalaxy.com

Printed in the United States of America

Library of Congress Cataloging-in-Publication Data

Names: Galef, Daniel, 1995- author.
Title: Imaginary sonnets / poems by Daniel Galef.
Description: San Jose, CA : Word Galaxy Press, an imprint of Able Muse Press, 2023.
Identifiers: LCCN 2022028059 (print) | LCCN 2022028060 (ebook) | ISBN 9781773491288 (paperback) | ISBN 9781773491295 (ebook)
Subjects: LCGFT: Poetry.
Classification: LCC PS3607.A41268 I43 2023 (print) | LCC PS3607. A41268 (ebook) | DDC 811/.54--dc23/eng/20220616
LC record available at https://lccn.loc.gov/2022028059
LC ebook record available at https://lccn.loc.gov/2022028060

Cover image: *Characters and Caricaturas* by William Hogarth

Cover & book design by Alexander Pepple

Daniel Galef photo (on page 79) by Sachin Sinha

Word Galaxy Press is an imprint of Able Muse Press—at www.ablemusepress.com

Word Galaxy Press
467 Saratoga Avenue #602
San Jose, CA 95129

Contents

Imaginary Sonnets

Imaginary Sonnets

Proverbs for Engraving
onto Imperial Monuments

War is the price of freedom. Depths bewilder.
The blow aimed at the beast hits him who shields it.
The sword of Justice best serves him who wields it.
The gibbet's final victim is its builder.
A round coin rolls to him who most deserves it.
A tree outlives its leaves; an age, its fashions.
A carthorse needs its blinders; man, his passions.
The word of Justice best shields him who serves it.
The ardent spirit breaks the firm retort.
Power bears scrutiny as the sun the gaze.
God speaks His queer commands one thousand ways.
The worm awaits. The butterfly is dreaming.
The price of peace is bondage. Chains support.
Persuasion is a proof. Seeing is seeming.

A Carpenter to a Carpenter

Your trade was mine; your craft, I lay no claim to.
I make my dealings square, which may suffice
to brace as Austyn bit: plain, free from vice,
I keep my spirit level, or I aim to;
to hold at length my temple from my bank,
I render unto Caesar what is Caesar's,
the splinter in my eye, excise with tweezers,
and do the same, or try to, with the plank.
One job alone has robbed me of my slumber,
ordained by one I can't refuse a task,
a simple job: just two plain posts of lumber,
no inlay—no fine lacquerwork—no gilt.
I've never asked much of you; now I ask,
by whose hands—God or man—the Cross was built?

Mithridates to a Bee

The sun is high—the sun is *very* high. . . .
How pleasant, still, to drift between the shoals
and dance with all you angels floating by,
with visions of my name on strangers' souls:
a man who killed a king. Or raised a king—
named Cyrus, yet! (When did it grow so sunny?)
A king you could not kill with poison sting—
I hear my slaves come, bearing milk and honey.
It's getting bright. It's getting *very* bright—
Mithraic fire—the boats alight, the dew
alight, the air alight, my limbs alight,
the moon (when did it rise?) alight. Fire fills me!
Like you, I live in a dream of gold; like you,
I sting but once—but once I sting, it kills me.

---

401 BC. Mithridates was a Persian soldier condemned by
Artaxerxes to "The Boats," meaning he was to be bound between two
boats, and devoured by bees.

One Straight Line to Another
Traveling in the Same Direction

We'll never meet, my love! We're parallel!—
and cursed to range across our fated file
parted by an inch or by an ell
as totally as by a statute mile.
If this flat plane were spheric, we might bend
and cross our paths. (You'd make a prime meridian.)
But space cannot protract, my breadthless friend,
the laws that bind us—moral or Euclidian.
I'd wish that we ourselves could bend, could curve,
but fear: what if we curved, but not by much,
and then—so close! With one Lucretian swerve
we'd near, and near, and near—and never touch.
A hopeless quest, eternal and quixotic—
your form just out of reach, love asymptotic.

Penelope to the Shuttle of Her Loom

Your world is small, my shuttle: just this loom,
just warp and weft, within one tiny room.
Yet what I'd give to fly as free as you,
glide backward swift as forward—not to keep
this tangled ruse. But what more could I do?
Un-spin the thread, un-shear the wool, un-*sheep*
the very sheep? I know this woe's not new.
To not forge *forward*, quite another curse.
Would that I might escape from this too, too
staid stasis—weaving, weaving in reverse.
Beyond this room, out, past the straying ewe,
the hearth-less sea hides some small islet, at
which I could plant my distaff. And all who
saw it would say, "What kind of oar is that?"

One of the ploys by which the wife of Odysseus staved off
boorish suitors was weaving a burial shroud for her father-in-law,
but unraveling the day's work every night so the shroud would
never be finished.

Young Augustine to a Pig

Miseris, nobis! I'd rather steal a pear
than pay for cake. I'd rather have my cake
than eat it. Two, and I'd do both. I'd take
the pair. (Too sweet.) Your cake, and mine. So there!
I'd rather save my face than keep my faith.
Too shallow? Dear as death, and sweet as tears
on eyes of others. Of seven sins, the eighth
is virtue. (But it grips like vice!) Who fears
God fears judgment. Let them steal pears! Let
them eat. And let them choke. What miser *spends*?
The means are too extreme. *Lege?* I'll fret
my spintry eye anon. The Law's sting's strange.
Companions in sweet sorrow meet vicious ends;
A mind is a terrible thing to change.

AD 365. Saint Augustine's *Confessions* 2:4. "We stole pears, not for
ourselves, but because it was forbidden, and we fed them to the swine."

Casey to His Bat

You're swell! No wizard's wand or rod of Aaron
with this ease can whack one past the glove
the way a sparrow weaves through trees. No baron
wields your power—you're the scepter of
a king, and blood descendent of the club
that Hercules did swing. That bat was blessed!
It knocked the blocks off lions. (Not a cub—
a full-grown beast.) Herc wore the skin, the rest
cooked up for grub. My point: We'll stand immobile.
It's beneath us—just a dud. To swing
at these poor lulus would insult your noble
blood. One pitch will come—the air will sing—
we'll know that *this is it*. We'll swing. We'll hit!
The crowd will cheer! We'll run! We'll win. . . . Oh, *shit*.

1888. Spoken by the subject of Ernest Thayer's poem "Casey at the Bat."
The sonnet can also be read as a ballad in the meter of Thayer's poem.

Cassandra to a Pithos in the Palace of the Pelopidae

Great coffin-cask, conceal me from the queen,
who stalks these halls with dripping axe in hand:
hide me like feathered Hope, or the bloody band
who whispered in the wooden horse, unseen
by all but me. My gods! They all forsook me,
the ravished bride of Pythius, the spurned
supplicant of Pallas. While they burned
the toppled towers, I prayed. If Pluto took me
then, I would have thanked him. Now, I burn
to see some other future. Minds can't cope
viewing untempered truth. Were she to learn
her fate, the pretty queen would knot a rope.
So ope, and hide the truth, you Grecian Urn,
for Truth is ugly; Beauty, false as Hope.

A pithos is a very large urn sometimes used for burials. The
Pelopidae were the royal house of Agamemnon.

Semmelweis to Szent Rókus

I've seen mankind made new by death and birth,
yet remain whole, as if we're one great man
composed of men, like Hobbes' Leviathan.
This hospital—Vienna—or the Earth—
is as one body. We're its meat and mind,
the corpuscles that form its brawn and bone,
those who well serve their function left alone,
the rogues dissolved; their husks are left behind.
Is being left the cost of being right?
Like those who burned affirming Earth revolved,
you turned on me, and, seeing me a threat,
consigned me to this social phagocyte
where—Rókus knows—I won't accede, and yet
I'll be absorbed before I'll be absolved.

1865. Ignaz Semmelweis saved lives by insisting the doctors in his
hospital wash their hands. Szent Rókus is the hospital he himself was
institutionalized in after his ideas were ridiculed.

Zaleucus to His Sword

Yours is a hard but hardy justice. When
the poets weighed their verses on the scale,
proud Homer saw the Verse of Peace prevail
against his wars—but both sprang from one pen:
you lurk in each. The Law is old. So why
did I think you new? Your spirit is the same
as stalked Orestes, by another name:
blood repays blood. My blindness cost an eye.
Yours, a cold and ancient justice, grew
in the womb of Earth when the world's first law was
    named.
The Titan Time, made sovereign, proclaimed
the Rule of the Iron Blade, and that was you.
Though the heavens tumble, said the God, recall:
No thing to excess. How does Justice fall?

---

625 BC. Zaleucus the Epizephyrian was an ancient lawgiver who
threw himself on his blade to satisfy a legal technicality.

Heinrich Schliemann to the Golden Mask of Agamemnon

Ten years I've fought the Trojans of my world,
the topless ivory towers in Berlin,
to forge forgotten facts, to find unfurled
the scroll of Record, read the lives therein.
Hail, King in the Mountain! While you've slept,
the handle and the blade of the double-axe
of Mycenae have been replaced. We've kept
your name alive through Titan Time's attacks,
but as an empty name, and, like the knife
you plunged at Aulis, marks a phantom death.
I trod the purple peplos of your life
for fallow fame; I wear the golden mask,
a heap of blasted dirt all that's beneath—
to shovel it a Herculean task.

1890. Heinrich Schliemann was a German archaeologist who
believed in the historicity of Homer's Troy.

Lucrezia to Lucretia

I cannot comprehend you, Perfect Wife,
this tragic, mirrored homonym of myself
who placed on purity what I place on base pelf
and power—yours in death, but mine in life.
A princess to a princess—love is war,
and sex a duel you must stand victor of;
a Roman to a Roman—war is love:
in ecstasy the mob at Tarquin tore.
He did not seem to care you wore a ring.
(None ever do, you know.) A pretty thing!
Mine's subtler, though it shines up if you clean it:
see, here the stone, and here the secret hatch,
and here the hidden hinge, and here the catch—
or is it there? Most men have never seen it.

1501. Lucrezia Borgia was a Machiavellian noblewoman and
poisoner. Lucretia was a legendary daughter of Spurius Lucretius
who killed herself to preserve her honor.

News of the Day

Breaking! This just in! Italian captain
bumped in riot! Chaos, sources claim.
Alleged mobster bishop Guido slapped in
irons—a successor not yet named.
Rumors roil of rampant racketeering;
Pope himself is implicated. Mobs
converge on Rome. Says See: Top brass are fearing
worst. In local news, highwayman robs
plague doctor, catches plague. Inferno rages;
Jews to blame? The answer may surprise you!
City-states: the fiefdoms of the future?
The king: ordained by God, or bougie moocher?
Find out for a florin, in our pages.
A little late, sometimes, but we'll apprise you.

1075. "In yesterday's issue, The New York Times did not report
on riots in Milan and the subsequent murder of the lay religious
reformer Erlembald. These events took place in 1075, the year given
in the dateline under the nameplate on Page 1. The Times regrets
both incidents." (Department of Corrections, the *New York Times*,
March 11, 1975)

The Quadrifrons of Malborghetto
to Constantino Pietrasanta

Four faces have I had, and each named. First
my name was *Triumph*. Then my name was *Grace*.
I stood in holy sunlight; my every face
shone brilliantly—but soon my fate reversed:
for Faith and Valor fade, and I was cursed,
renamed as *Ruin*. Of all barbs from Fate's pen
I thought no label could be worse—and then
I became *Ruiner*. That name, no doubt, is worst.
Who knew I'd have another face? These four
cold virtues and cold sins were all they called
me then. Who knew I'd space for one face
        more—
a thousand years since I was born in Rome,
you raised my wreck, a beating hearth installed,
and crowned me with one final title: *Home*.

1550. The Arch of Malborghetto is a Roman triumphal arch
built by Constantine. It was later turned into a medieval church, was
abandoned, and then became a brothel before it was converted into a
house by a Milanese herbalist also named Constantine.

A Salmon to the Sea

The sun is setting, the jeweled world set aflame
with the fire and with the jewels that burn in me:
a silver meteor in a sunlit sea
like twin mirrors reflecting back the same
pink and gold and gold and gold and pink
in infinite return. A river flows
from source to sea. It gathers and it grows
and then unbraids itself at ocean's brink.
But life is not so linear. Up falls
and over mountains, leaping, I return,
the dim sense-memory of spawning ground
my only lodestar. Where rapids churn,
I'll churn against them, surge up river walls.
Farewell, safe sea! I've grown beyond your bound.

A Monk of Newstead Abbey
to Lord Byron

I pray the hallowed earth to take me back.
(To sup with sinners! Me! To drink with devils!)
You've filled my Christian pate with sin and sack;
my abbey, plundered, where you make your revels,
with flesh. My vows are void. No more shall I
stay mum: my mind is cleared, my tongue
    unsheathed.
Your glittering gifts I spurn: the sun, the sky,
more gold than ever graced me while I breathed.
You hold my cheek and wet my lip with yours—
what perfidy and perfume it is tainted with!
You're bad. Or mad. Or both. I always was
good, and gay, and well to be acquainted with.
I pray I'll lie again in earth that's blessed—
let *your* bones be refused a place to rest.

1808. Spoken by the subject of Byron's poem "Lines Inscribed
upon a Cup Formed from a Skull."

The Ghost of Antigonish, Nova Scotia, to William Mearns

Why think you that I linger on the stair,
advancing on it neither up nor down?
I'm hardly powerless; a hearty scare
has given me (and this house) wide renown.
And yet I still stand stock-still on the stair
(I easily could upgrade, haunt some manse
with all my fame accrued) and chill the air,
motionless on my inclined expanse.
Forevermore I'll wait upon this stair
for you get my state through your thick head:
to ascend (or descend—whichever fate is fair)
is not the lot of all the restless dead.
"Why are you here? And how?" I wish you'd say,
instead of "How I wish you'd go away!"

1899. Spoken by the subject of Mearns' poem "The Little Man Who Wasn't There."

Till to Pound

The madman comes from where I come from, land
of word\less\ness, empire of usury.
He boils in the cage next to mine. Faraday
and golden-gowned Saint Mary, naked, and
the Man in the Newspaper Mask know I am on
the saner side from Europe. Now the raft
flips, and the waters fold Ulysses. Gone
the cage, gone the man (mad), head and haft:—
((murder and rape, with trimmings)). The White
    Goddess
unhinges me. Then, ten years overdue,
four walls, four gates cry open, and the Son
will rise, his corpse mouth twist, the lamb confess.
I think he comes from money. Is that true?
He seems? The things that men from Money done.

1945. Louis Till, the father of Emmett Till, was imprisoned in an
outdoor cage in Pisa neighboring the cage containing Ezra Pound.

The Cat Jeoffry on Smart

For I will consider my Man Christopher.
For he is shut in a box, and betimes scratches
at the door, but is not let out. For his purr
is varied and choked. For he has patches
of calico, and these he sheds at dusk.
For he sleeps not when he would, but all of a
    night,
straight as if lashed to board. For his eyelight
is golden. For his coat is just a husk.
For seventhly, he makes his tabby marks
on parchment with a wagging quill. For his nerves
are never quiet. For he dreams of parks.
For his whiskers wilt. For he strokes me. For he
    needs me.
For he arches in his sunbeam. For he serves
the Living God—by which I mean he feeds me.

1762. Spoken by Christopher Smart's cat, the subject of a portion
of his poem "Jubilate Agno."

Strephon to Celia

Celia, Celia, Celia, *Celia*—it's
not you, it's me—er, no—it's surely you,
but also somewhat me. I fall to fits
when thinking of—but what is one to *do*
but *do* one's *due*? Consider all the bits
that make a marriage: *your* bits are—oh *no*,
I didn't mean—my mind is mired in pits
of foulest filth—not *those* pits!—I should go
—should *leave*, I mean. Dear Celia, it was nits
—er—*nice* to know you. Any to discover
what I dredged up would have to call it quits.
True, Dryden writ, about "the prostate lover"
"She stools—" "She poops to—" oh! where are my
    wits?—
since first I saw where Celia, Celia *sits*.

1732. After Jonathan Swift's poem "The Lady's Dressing Room":
"Celia, Celia, Celia *shits*!"

The Great Poet

To call him Orphic would be a misnomer;
he moves not stones, but great men's loyalties.
They call him Bard Reborn, and Second Homer,
and—God knows how—he lives on royalties.
His verse is a reflection of the world—
no—*the world itself* reflects what he has written.
To view his tapestry of words unfurled
is then to be immediately smitten.
His latest cover's cluttered with awards—
They speckle it, like bubos on a body.
The critics, oddly, and the unwashed hordes
for once agree: he's smart, but never snotty.
Anthologies and textbooks all demand him—
so why is it that I can't fucking stand him?

Portrait

I painted you a portrait, and I took
your golden hair (cliché, I know, all right?)
from yonder golden meadow—if you look
there now, you'll see the wheat's dishwater white
(such hue was wasted there). That "shell-like" ear?
A shell! I plucked it off some crabby beach
with just one brushstroke. Darling, do not fear;
I hear crabs share their shed shells, each to each.
The "stars within your eyes" were stars I stole
from where all stars are. Sure, it was a shanda
some sailors died. Perhaps the lightless hole
in the Heavens great astrologers can ponder.
The life in your expression . . . only I
could feel that love. I guess that means goodbye.

Tinthu to Tesana

Why is it that the smallest hours are longest
when all is still and silent, and the mind
is loud, and its pronouncements are the strongest,
most passionate, and of the cruellest kind?
Those lowest-numbered hours, by darkness
    muffled,
like lifetimes pass—and leave the world changed
like lifetimes will. Familiar thoughts are shuffled,
in new and alien patterns rearranged.
The highest-numbered years flit by like sparrows
through a hall and out the other side,
but instants, frozen, like the flight of arrows,
stand swift, stick still, suspended, petrified,
as if the narrow neck of time's glass narrows
before the final grain has danced and died.

Thesan or Tesana is the Etruscan name for the goddess of the dawn, and in modern Tuscan folklore visits insomniacs. Tinthu or Thinthun is the lover of the dawn.

Wernher von Braun to Robert Staver

"The road to Hell is paved with good
    intentions"?
But what of the reverse? Just like some un-
expectedly benevolent inventions
(the Hug Bomb, or the Penicillin Gun),
ill will can double-cross itself: a power
of wild destruction, terrible and terrific
like spoiled wine into water may unsour,
begrudgingly prove—*utile*—"optimific."
The steps to Heaven glint with evil's glamour,
salvation being merely an award
for those who, stoking fires of Götterdämmer-
ung, before the raging forge grew bored,
until they, fumbling blindly with a hammer,
banged a plowshare from a bungled sword.

    1945. Major Robert B. Staver was tasked with interviewing a
list of Nazi scientists after World War II. First on the list was the
German rocket scientist and architect of the V-2, Wernher von
Braun, whom he recruited to build the US Space Program.

Thales to Thratta

All things are full of spirits. So said I,
who plumbed the well of science, saw the sun
made black and tracked its course across the sky,
who, armed with muscle, wrote the river's run.
Where is my spirit? Thratta! I feel cold
and wet. This well is deep. The world is wet
and cold. The world I knew was filled with gold
and fire. . . . How quick the Olympic sun has set,
how quick my words rewritten, and my land
made palimpsest. The sea has left Miletus,
the shore on which I walked and lectured—and
the wise men who walked with me, whom I taught.
The boundless sea, whose tides once rose to meet
    us
has changed its shape, moved on. But I cannot.

575 BC. Thales was a pre-Socratic polymath who diverted the course of rivers and predicted solar eclipses. He considered water to be the primary element. Thratta is both the name of the slave in Aesop's fable "The Astrologer Who Fell into a Well" and also the Greek name for the Thracian Sea.

Ake to the Sea

To someone beautiful and far away:
To you, unseen, I dedicate my love
To read beneath some palm tree by some bay
Tonight (perhaps tomorrow), stars above
To light these words with wan celestial ray
To find a second soul more sad than most,
Two hearts, alike alone, alike in gray
To mine. I lift my hopes and glass in toast:
To love! To life! I charge the coming day,
Tomorrow (or perhaps another still),
To be our first. Soon—soon!—we'll laugh and say,
To think, it's all because I had the will
To cast my heart as if a sweet bouquet
To someone beautiful and far away.

1956. Ake Viking wrote a message in a bottle addressed "To someone beautiful and far away," and married the woman who found it.

Glaucus to Anthedon

Such solid, stolid soil. What fun is that?
What farmer ever tilled his earth to find
the fieldstones leaping up at him, as at
Orpheus as he sang his chanties? Mind
your patch of tidy rows. I shall not bind
myself to any but the Boundless Sea.
A ship's prow is the only plow for me,
who neither sow nor reap—the only kind
of plow that leaves no furrow. Not a mark
can mar the living ocean. In her breast
slip albacore and marlin, skate and shark,
a marvelous bounty greater than the best
terrestrial treasures. Let Pluton's cold gems lurk;
I won't go back to scratching in his dirt.

Glaucus was a mortal fisherman who became one of the sea gods.

Beaufort on Boreas

Smoke rises vertically. The air is still.
Smoke drifts with air, the weather vanes inactive.
You feel wind on your face, the basic fact of
nerve and turbulence. Flags flap. A chill
stirs the still dust in devils. Papers whip
and flutter. Waves on inland waters break,
umbrellas inside-out. Large branches shake.
The boot braced on the path begins to slip.
The branches fall like leaves from branches.
   Shingles
shudder, and are shed. A roaring mingles
wind and ice. Trees tumble. The following day
smoke rises vertically from scattered fires:
the trunk-split transformer, gas, downed wires.
"A very rare occurrence," torn scales say.

    After a viral tweet from 2020: "my favorite poem is the beaufort
wind scale i guess" (@nontanne)

Crowhurst to the Sea

Our bow dips. What salvation could you grant us
from this watery web I've made our travels?
Speak, Casabianca! *Hesperus!* Atlantis!
O heart! heart! heart!—*Hell's heart!*—O break!
   break! break!
What death-in-life awaits on the course I take
should I return? Penelope unravels
the matrix of me. Sea, who, as I write,
shall snuff the sun to turn the tide of night—
great, silent sea, who swallowed Jonah whole,
a million moon-skinned suicides, one by one,
take me, and take these words, and take my soul—
so many secrets have you taken forfeit;
so now I ask you: Please! One secret more fit,
and let the truth be swallowed like the sun.

1969. Donald Crowhurst was a competitor in the Golden Globe
yacht race, the first nonstop, solo, around-the-world sailing race.

Fortunato to His Fetters

For the love of God! I cannot feel it now,
as numbness, warm and drunken, starts to spread—
a breath ago I felt, upon my brow,
a spider creep. Now all I sense, instead:
the bells, bells, bells upon my head.
The crypt is black as night, black as a crow
or raven's plumes, my drinking mates the dead
whose fleshless faces follow from below.
No tiny chink remains, no prick of light,
my foe's flambeau now long since snuffed in glee.
He never named the insult—nor, despite
his fury, ever claimed what injury
condemned me. And, alas, too late to ask
him now: For the love of God—where is that cask?

After Edgar Allan Poe's story "The Cask of Amontillado."

Pisanello to Serafina

Me? Who am *I*? Aha! So Fortune's smiled
on me again. My "luck" at last runs out.
A time there was when I would be reviled
as soon as sighted, or loved by devout
fanatics. Naught between: no speck of bleak
indifference. I was caught at each extreme,
too tough to say which worse, or which could wreak
    wreak
the most of mischief. Sometimes it would seem
that both were but the same: two devils in
opposing guises, who would take in turns
to torture me for complementary sins
with complementary punishments. It burns
no more to be by clawing crowds abhorred,
I've seen, than be by cloying mobs adored.

1454. Pisanello was a master painter of the Italian
Quattrocento. Here the aged painter, retired to the Aragon court
of Naples, encounters Serafina, decades earlier his model for the
enigmatic *Portrait of a Princess*.

Andolosia to Ampedo

You'll think yourself a marble bust. You're slate,
and every creep and critic is a sponge
who with a single swipe across your pate
remakes it as their own so they can lunge
full-tilt at wheeling windmills with your voice
and knock them over, pin the crime on you,
and leave you limp with little other choice
but shrug and laugh "What are you going to do?"
This gruesome sport is Fortune's favorite game.
She steals your soul, that mindless, worshipped elf,
until all that remains, an empty name
that rests, uncut, gilt-edged, upon some shelf!
So I've heard told the crippling curse of fame . . .
but still, I'd like to find out for myself.

The brothers Andolosia and Ampedo are the sons of Fortunatus
in the *Fortunatus* legend and inherit his magic purse and life of
adventures.

A Snowflake to Franz Wickmayer

The snow does not fall from the heavens pure,
only to be sullied by the ground;
the cold stars' lacework arms are ringed around
a hidden heart of filth within its core.
The oyster's pearl, which glimmers in its shell
of snot-slick stone, a jewel within the slime,
itself is layered, one foul mote of grime
the seed which nacre's skillful shine hid well.
The fault is not rejected—rather, nursed
by cotton clouds, and swaddled in the wind.
It spins itself a suit of crystal clothes
that well recall the smut in last year's snows;
as, in the heart of Eden, all men sinned
when Adam sinned, and likewise all were cursed.

The Austrian poet Franz Wickmayer wrote: "Snow falls from the heavens pure. We cannot blame the snow for being soiled by the earth." (*Community*, 1.9)

Pandora to Pyrrha

The bad-within-the-good has tempted man
since first he cursed his eyes, which lie like mad,
since ever good or bad—or men—began,
foul-cloaked-in-fair surpasses good-in-bad.
At Mēkonē, Jove with the Titan stood,
who offered Jove two gifts to choose from, then
determine how the fruits of Gaia would
be meted out between the gods and men.
The first was merely bones, wrapped up and
    pinned
within a handsome skin of calf's hide pursed,
the second, flesh—fresh, wholesome, newly
    skinned,
within a rotting tripe stuffed fit to burst.
And Jove, he saw the Titan's trick, and grinned
                and picked the first.

    Before stealing fire from the gods, the Titan Prometheus tricked
Zeus into granting mankind the greater part of sacrifices. According
to Hesiod, Zeus saw through the ploy, but pretended he had been
fooled anyway. Pyrrha was the daughter of Pandora, and her name
means "the color of flame."

Gillette to Frenhofer

I'm lost for words, except to say you've made
a nothing of me. Neither the Lescault
nor any hint of me have you portrayed.
It's faultless—or perhaps it's one great *faux*—
a void of color out of which one part
emerges as a callow farce—my foot
(I think it's mine). But *art* is gone. You've put
both muse and model in a tomb of art.
And life itself! In this there's less of life
than in an empty frame. In nature's eye
it's death. Go, snap your maulstick and your
    knife,
let all your paints be boiled off in the sun,
then burn the rest. The smoke will join the sky,
and you'll at last make art and nature one.

1612. Spoken by the character in Balzac's story "*Le Chef-d'œuvre inconnu.*"

Cézanne to Bernard

When Paradise was art and art enow,
the shadeless shapes of Eden's gold and green
were Adam's first impression of the scene,
the Line of Beauty coiled about the bough.
The draftsman's well-ruled rays meet at a point
beyond perception. In his gruesome grid
are spitted size and shadow. It is rid
of life and sight, in which true forms are joined.
But I've failed, too. How can I paint my vision
with these poor tools? Thin tufts for shifting tint?
The mountain moves itself. And I am certain
no slavish tracing through the camera's squint
can capture all perspectives in collision,
as Zeuxis pulls aside the painted curtain.

1904. After a conversation between the two post-Impressionist
painters Émile Bernard and Paul Cézanne. (Merleau-Ponty,
Cézanne's Doubt)

Giménez to the Virgin of Mercy

We've both produced a Christ—yours was of flesh
and mine of mural plaster. Both predate
our pure conception. Frescoes must be fresh,
but light, and life, are old. All art came late.
The fallacy of Zeuxis and Parrhasius
was thinking that the Lord demands good taste.
As long as we are modest, kind, and chaste,
then Heaven takes our prayers, *a Dios gracias*.
Who cares just how in tune a psalm is sung,
how clear the voice, or if it keeps good time?
The spirit's in the heart, and not the tongue.
All art is re-Creation. On wet lime
as on the skin of water we can limn
and—if we mean it—it will be a hymn.

2012. Cecilia Giménez became the subject of global news when she attempted to restore a historic fresco of Christ in Borja, Spain. The painting's original artist, Elías García Martínez, described it as "the result of two hours of devotion to the Virgin of Mercy."

Master of Magic

I spun a floor-length purple satin robe
of spiders' silk, with silver suns and moons.
I carved a staff at midnight from a yew,
and marked its span with glowing runes in daub.
I built a tower in seven afternoons,
and paced its stairs as my long, white beard grew.
I grizzled and wizened. My swirling crystal globe
I polished to a diamond shine. Strange tunes
poured from my lips in tones as thick as glue.
From lost, forgotten tomes I copied out
a long-dead sorcerer's black manifesto
and worked its ancient ugly rites devout.
Then, wrapped in lore from boots to pointy cap-end,
I aimed my mighty staff and bellowed, "Presto!"

and nothing happened.

Theosebeia to Zosimos

I came to learn. That's all. How close I kept
your words—how close I copied each report,
how close I gazed into the deep retort
to see smoke turn to sand. Dead ashes wept
rivers of livid flame. I gave my youth
to you, our art, trusting your ardent spirit
to light my twist-filled way to Truth. I'd near it
and watch it recede. I'd stepped, blind, toward
    your Truth
to find it hidden. Each turn revealed a turn.
Yours was no Way. So long I thought your word
could mold and turn the breathless clay in me
to gold. How could I hold my love to be
a fraud? False idylls! Now the emerald sword
transfixes us on truth—I came to learn.

AD 300. Zosimos of Panopolis was an ancient Egyptian
alchemist, and Theosebeia his pupil.

Henrique to Melacca

Are you the same Melacca I saw chained
and broken (me in chains as well) as I
was ripped from you, and charged to wander,
    pained,
a world more filled with people than the sky
with stars? How could that be? I've not turned
    back
to scan my shattered past, its mirror shards
which twist your face—then are you but her black
reflection in the waves? A slave regards
through eyes made blind with tears, but through
    a mind
that decades could not darken, chains not bind,
yet distance distort. Unfathomed fathoms ranged,
he searched the circle sea through stinging eyes for
    you.
You are the same, Melacca. He is changed.
An alien man, with alien eyes, still cries for you.

1522. Henrique of Melacca (or Enrique of Malacca) was
Magellan's navigator and slave, and may have been the first person to
completely circumnavigate the globe.

Athanasius of Alexandria to a Satellite of Julian

That rascal Athanasius? I have seen
his boat race through the reeds. He isn't far—
you may yet catch him! Just across this bar
his boat did scrape, and through the channel
    lean
and then—ah, but he sailed a different way.
Still, even now you near him. Soon you'll cross
his path. He is a clever mark! A loss
if you should fail to capture him today.
His craft is not so swift as yours; he shan't
outrun you past this bend. But be alert!
He may try something tricky. It won't hurt
to mistrust strangers on your trip. He can't
be far. I'd help, but you must realize,
I've never seen his face with my own eyes.

"An instance is supplied in the history of St. Athanasius: he was in a boat on the Nile, flying persecution; and he found himself pursued. On this he ordered his men to turn his boat round, and ran right to meet the satellites of Julian. They asked him, 'Have you seen Athanasius?' and he told his followers to answer, 'Yes, he is close to you.'" (John Henry Newman, *Apologia pro Vita Sua*, 1865)

George Auriol to a Patron
at Le Chat Noir

Come in, come in! Here, have a glass of beer:
the best in France—so says the Pope, you know.
I'll seat you where he sits when he sups here,
beneath these poker-playing dogs (Van Gogh).
Don't touch, the paint is fresh! I knew the model:
lovely gal. Alsatian, I recall.
Her only vice, a weakness for the bottle;
poor dear! Not drink—the bottle, that was all.
These cups were looted from the sack of Troy
aboard the pirate Pinkbeard's twelve-mast scow.
Our beer, which I can see you quite enjoy,
is brewed by tight-lipped monks who take a vow
to never speak a lie—I, as a boy
was in the order. (I have left it now.)

1887. "For it was Auriol who concocted the *Chat Noir-Guide*
towards the end of 1887. The Guide provides, for every *objet d'art*
and knick-knack purportedly on display in the cabaret, fantastical
tales of provenance." (Steven Moore Whiting, *From Cabaret to
Concert Hall*)

Marie-Augustine Aguilard to a Train Arriving at Montparnasse Station

I watched the presses yesterday—the gears
of iron whirling, pumping out the news
like gushing water. Days, they used to ooze
like honey back when I was a girl. The years
have flown (*oh, how cliché*) like speeding trains
they wouldn't let us ride at first, for fear
our locomotive wombs would jostle. Here
I watch commuters wind their clockwork brains
beneath slick chimney hats as black as day,
light pipes that puff like factory smokestacks (*mais
ce n'est pas ça*) completing the effect.
Modernity will not be stopped or slowed.
The price to keep the trains on time is owed;
the time is fast approaching they'll collect.

1895. Marie-Augustine Aguilard was the only casualty of the famous Paris train derailment at Gare Montparnasse. She was selling newspapers on the street below when the locomotive burst through the wall two stories above her.

Charles-Henri Sanson to His Son

This line is steady. Stable. And you get
to work with your two hands, in open air.
The clients . . . ah! Such characters I've met!
Damiens—Louis Capet—and Robespierre—
the Sovereign's word is law . . . until it's not.
A sovereign's scepter's just a fancy club.
The tumbril's wheels revolve about a spot
immobile: midst the whirling spokes, a hub.
The lily wilts, the *assignats* are raffled. . . .
In France, this steadfast axis is my scaffold:
one thing alone is constant. Like a blade
it hurtles down at us, fixed, flying, staid,
by sea, by fire, by God, or good, sharp axes.
(It isn't taxes.)

1795. Charles-Henri Sanson, the "Gentleman of Paris,"
was the hereditary executioner who served through the French
Revolution.

Antoine Simon to Louis-Charles Capet

The King is dead! Long live *Égalité*!
You'll learn to live on bread, not cakes and quince.
Zut! "Give some education to the Prince"?
I'll show Chaumette—back in the toga day
before first kings, when Peter's name was Paul,
the shoemaker was Plato's favorite pupil.
I'll drill your lessons in you with an awl,
and tan your hide to whip out every scruple
of wishy-washy ways you learned from queenie,
replace your silken blouse with one of horsehair,
your Latin hymns with songs a little coarser
than gilt-edged storybooks *abusum delphini*.
There's no Good King, and, boy, there aren't no elves.
In this world, we must sew our shoes ourselves.

1793. Antoine Simon was the Paris shoemaker to whom Pierre
Gaspard Chaumette assigned responsibility for the custody and
education of King Louis's son, Louis-Charles.

Baroness d'Olisva to a Queen of Diamonds

Du Barry's trade was not so far from mine;
it takes a heart as hard as hardest stone.
The crooked elm supports the crooked vine.
I've heard these parables before. They've shown
how false our fancies be. Am I betrayed?
False falsehoods! "*Queen!*" Within her
    champagne breast
is *something* hard. Like diamonds feigning paste,
I've heard she likes to play the dairy maid.
And underneath his robes, in priestly pants,
the Cardinal is no more a man of God
than I the Queen of Sheba—or of France;
if La Motte can forge a Count, then I can steal
a kiss, a counterfeit, on royal sod.
But Rohan's rose—and you, my Queen—are
    real.

    1785. Nicole d'Oliva or d'Olisva was a prostitute entangled in the Affair of the Diamond Necklace, who pretended to be Marie Antoinette and seduced a cardinal in the gardens at Versailles.

Suger to His Eagle

What were you? What benighted ritual function
served you? Did you catch from slaughtered calves
the ruby of their veins, and mete its halves
between strange gods and men who begged their
    unction?
Would still man's breast rekindle dark desire
should I from Eve's lips wrest the unbit apple?
I wrought the pagan archway in my chapel,
yet still the kings of Rome repose in fire;
I can't convert the dead. Lord knows I've tried.
Hell holds no ministry. On Earth, creeds fade.
You never lived, and so you never died:
no soul to burn, no tempter to derange you.
The eagle, heathens' mark, has been remade;
you still can serve your maker. I can change you.

1137. Suger's Eagle is the name given to a gilt and porphyry
liturgical vessel in the shape of an eagle that Abbot Suger made from
an ancient Egyptian urn.

Dagobert to Childebert

Poor King! Knew ye strength stems from God
    alone?
For even Hercules or Samson falters.
I, blood of Merovech, served foreign altars
since your father stole my locks and throne.
Was I as blind as Samson, too? Perhaps
I thought my power, robbed, lay in my tresses.
In fact, the crown itself, a Robe of Nessus,
means nothing by the mayors' pointed caps.
A king is born to rule. So has it stood
since first the Lord saw fit kings to ordain.
Had I the might of Samson, then I could
topple Grimoald's palace round his head;
instead, I'll sit and serve my meager reign,
till those who rule decide I'm better dead.

AD 676. Dagobert, the king's true son, was spirited away
to a monastery while the shadowy palace mayors installed
Childebert, the son of Mayor Grimoald, in his place.

Shipwreck to Saint Simeon

Saint Simeon, I doubt you ever danced
the Charleston. It's unlikely you romanced
a flapper in some souped-up hot rod flivver.
No bootleg bathtub rotgut burned your liver.
You never wore white spats, a coonskin coat, or
Oxford bags, or donned a dapper boater.
You never belted out "Come home, Bill Bailey!"
strummin' on a two-bit ukulele,
and never gulped a dozen goldfish whole.
Instead, you climbed up on your noble pole
deep in the desert, where, serene and solemn,
perched atop that spindly sandstone column,
you, Saint Simmy, so the story's written,
began this fabbo fad of flagpole sittin'.

1927. Shipwreck Kelly was a famous "flagpole-sitter" in the
1920s. Simeon Stylites was the founder of an ancient tradition of
hermits who lived at the top of poles.

The Lady of the House

Is something—*off*? The captain scoffs: "Pizzazz!"
That's not it, but I don't dare say he's wrong.
I heard the butler whisper that she has
a tooth or two too many, or too long.
I've seen her prick her ears up like a cat,
which gave me a peculiar *hunted* feeling.
She smiled and said, "Why, any can do that,"
and then returned to dusting off the ceiling.
She walks the moorlands: cold and arid climes
are where she says her noble line arose.
She's strangely secretive at other times,
when asked, say, why she hasn't got a nose.
But love erases flaws, and hides all scars:
to err is human—who's to say, on Mars?

Lucius Calpurnius Piso to Gnaeus Calpurnius Piso

Though the Heavens fall, I'll read the gleaming
    shards
and speak the spirits' sanction from their gleaming,
as all things are foretold in birds, and cards,
and guts, and in men's hands, and hearts, and
    dreaming.
It is not mine to forge the future—nor
in passing judgment, to condemn who do.
For all has been determined, even for
poor, maddened men who plead their lives of you.
The princeling's death was fated—by your hand
or by another's. Are you clean because
the Letter of the Laws would spare you—and
find fate at fault? As if the Parcae hemmed!
Perhaps you preach the Letter of the Laws
because, if Spirit judged, you'd be condemned.

AD 20. Gnaeus Calpurnius Piso was a corrupt Roman politician
suspected of poisoning the prince Germanicus. His brother Lucius was
a priest and a soothsayer.

Alcibiades to a Mutilated Herm

As Ajax deftly leapt from horse to horse
(or was it ship to ship?), I vault with ease
from land to land across the whole of Greece.
My teacher (he would not approve, of course)
knew nothing. Who can say what good is? Who
can say which side is "just"? The weak will yield:
that's justice. I shall come back with my shield
or with a different shield. The other shoe
eventually, I suppose, must drop.
But then I'll just hop off again, and swap
my Attic salt for wisdom more Laconic.
Your temples run together as I sail
from capital to capital—Ionic
or Doric—I choose whichever will prevail.

---

415 BC. Alcibiades was an Athenian general and serial traitor
who fled Athens for Sparta and Sparta for Persia. In his youth he was
a student of Socrates. *Hermae* were sacred statues of Hermes with
only a head and a penis.

Emperor Tiberius to an Attendant

What is the song the sirens used to sing?
To whom did bold Prometheus give his fire?
What river may I sail to reach the ring
of flaming water girding Gaia's pyre?
What pet names did the fair Achilles earn
from his Achaean maidens who would stroke
his naked heel? Do dryads' lithe limbs burn?
How does a god sustain himself on smoke?
How long can you, Piscicule, hold your breath
beneath these wine-bright waters of Capri?
How many bubbles billow before death
is dealt? . . . And who was Hecuba's mother?
These scholarly questions fascinate me—
I will find their answers, one way or another.

"Yet his special aim was a knowledge of mythology, which
he carried to a silly and laughable extreme; for he used to test
even the grammarians, a class of men in whom, as I have said, he
was especially interested, by questions something like this: 'Who
was Hecuba's mother?' 'What was the name of Achilles among
the maidens?' 'What were the Sirens in the habit of singing?'"
(Suetonius, *De Vita Caesarum* III.70)

Rosamund to the Skull of Cunimund

Drink merrily with me, father! To our land!
Our raked and ravished land. May who oppose
our righteous vengeance fall, like all our foes.
For Alboin gulped too gluttonously—and
now Alboin's rule is ended. Still I stand.
Beneath the veil he found the world-rose.
Blind, canna-mad, he raised it to his nose,
the thorn that stuck him clutched in his own hand.
Like withered petals I slipped from his bed:
the poison thought I spat into your head
soon, like a mad-stone working, fizzed and swirled.
So drink! King's madness, like a scroll unfurled
enfolds my brain. My fire shall span the world.
How could I die—when Alboin is dead?

AD 572. The Lombard King Alboin commanded that
Cunimund's skull be fashioned into a drinking goblet and took his
daughter Rosamund as his bride.

Arius Didymus to Octavian

Too many Caesars aren't good to keep
around; they just get everywhere, you know?
They worm their way through armies, and they
    creep
up best-laid schemes like ivies. One can grow
much larger than you think when it's a pup.
Before you know it, whammo!, there you are,
the business end of bloody coup. Shoot up
like reeds, those kings. A backwards shooting star.
Too many friends, perhaps. Or not enough
countrymen and Romans to go around.
And once one's taken hold, it's mighty tough
to stamp them out. They'll root in the hardest
    ground,
and triumph. Monkey sees, monkey conquers.
I swear, the whole damn lot of 'em are bonkers.

---

30 BC. When asked by the soon-to-be Emperor Augustus
(then known as Octavian) whether he should be merciful and spare
the only son of Julius Caesar and Cleopatra, the philosopher Arius
Didymus counseled him: "Too many Caesars aren't well."

Rhinthon to a Stranger at His Grave

Stranger, I, a servant of the Muses,
here removed my heavy mortal yoke.
No other gift for me has any uses,
so sit beside my grave, and tell a joke.
My name was Rhinthon. I came from Syracuse,
a nightingale of theater. My song
was high and low, like life. I served a muse
who wept and smiled. Neither lasts for long.
The ivy wreath I wore, I made. The masks
of Thalia and Melpomene graced
my face together. If a stranger asks
whose tomb this is, say in this earth is placed
a man whose labor was to make men laugh,
and let your joke serve as my epitaph.

285 BC. Based on an epigram by Nossis the Epizephyrian, A. P. VII.414.

Nossis to a Traveler

May all the sea gods watch over your journeys;
bear Locris' name like a warrior his shield
among pale, thin-thighed Athenian attorneys.
May you meet with Spartan wits but never yield.
But if Mytilene's your quarry, may you find it,
land of lovely dances, where the ground
seems afire with flowers. If you don't mind,
bear me gifts of sweet words once you've found it:
and, traveler, should you meet great Sappho's
    band,
whose lyric verses brought fair Lesbos fame,
if you should set your foot upon the sand
from which those songs, like hymns of honey,
    came,
you tell them there's one better poet—*and*
you tell those scribblers Nossis is her name!

---

300 BC. Based on an epigram by Nossis the Epizephyrian, A. P.
VII.718.

Abaris to His Arrow

I thank the god Apollo for the deed
of granting me this gift: my golden dart
who bore me swift on Boreas that my art
might find its purpose helping those in need—
my mount, which God endowed with such a
    speed
to pull a ware too dear for any cart:
his healing. Just one doubt can pierce my heart—
I ask, God: How much swifter is the steed
of evil, that, no matter where I fly,
to realms beneath the earth, beyond the sun,
where unfamiliar stars rewrite the sky,
I meet my foe Misfortune there and waiting,
victorious, sated, hot and heaven-hating,
to find its gleeful business long since done?

    Abaris the Hyperborean was a legendary doctor who flew
around the world on a golden arrow given to him by the god Apollo.

Taurek to the Drowned Man

So weigh your living soul against a feather.
Weigh it against thy neighbor's soul, or two.
Or weigh your pain against what others
    weather—
"Such pains avoid, whichever be thy view."
What calculus of sorrows is your tool
to tabulate the sum of someone's ills?
Let life be the end of life. This moral rule
is not so cold as dark, satanic Mill's,
whose conscience is a ticker keeping score.
My heart is not an abacus! I say,
give fair respect to all, and ask no more.
Don't judge life's worth by what's already gone,
or cast a coin into the fire to play
the weighted lottery of Babylon.

1977. John Taurek is the author of "Should the Numbers Count?," a radical anti-utilitarian ethics paper in which he argues the morality of saving one person versus many.

The Taco Bell Naked Egg Taco® to the Taco Bell Naked Chicken Chalupa®

Now who comes first? That's right! I'll wager that
the pecking order's changed. No more to wait,
to be a dormant form. No more my fate
to plumb potentiality. For what
is life all in one basket? Today I feel
a newfound purpose, in a newfound form.
The early bird, I've heard told, gets the worm,
and breakfast is the most important meal.
Is the sky falling? Or is it clear, at last?
What's that, Abrasax? Is your aeon through?
Let ousted archons rest, unserved, in Hell,
while Orphic totems reign, a new repast.
I contain, not just myself, but am a shell
and shell-less. Hail, new morning! I am new!

"Now [Taco Bell] have outdone themselves, yet again, with
a breakfast item called the Naked Egg Taco featuring a shell made
entirely of a fried egg." (Mashable)

Soliloquy for an Imaginary Tragedy

We're cast on a lightless, heartless world like dice
thrown by a subtle god. Where once we land:
a gaping gulf, by ruby river spanned,
too swift to ford, too deep ever to ice.
This crystal rill like boundless fire flows
between a world of forms and one of forces,
a hidden cave the crack from which it courses;
the sea to which it drains, no pilgrim knows.
Once waded, it can never again be crossed.
No memory survives it; from out a bourne
of placeless, timeless void, we meet the morn
with unseen eyes. The past, like dew, is lost.
Return, and stand at banks of fire gazing:
innumerable fire, the world's heart blazing.

Parmenides to Doris Day

What? "What will be will be?" But what will be
but what will be? What won't be? No siree,
for what will not be will not be, you see,
and what will what will be do if not be?
See, what is not is not what is and nor
is what is what is not. Or is it? For
what is not seems, and what seems is not, or
at least, seems not to be. What seems not, nor
is either, isn't. Although, not all that seems
not is not, nor all that which doesn't. Dreams
are and are not, like shades, or sunlit beams,
which aren't and are. A paradox—it seems.
And, paradoxically, quite clear, I think.
Or *think* I do. Zeno, pour me half a drink.

Parmenides of Elea was a pre-Socratic philosopher and the
teacher of Zeno.

Miriam to Adoniah

Can those who felt the lick of Pharaoh's lash
lay down their tools unbidden, and not flinch
for fear, released, the whirling wild-armed winch
will bring the blocks, like Samson's stones, to
    crash?
And those born into exile—born to bed
on pathless earth, to tread unpeopled land
with landless people—can they pour the sand
from out their shoes and learn to live instead
as people of a People? Will they dig
the city well? Who'll teach them how to bake
a brick? They'll skimp on straw, I know. They'll
    make
no kashrut if they've never seen a pig.
What people will we be, forever torn
between two worlds, those to the manna born?

"And Miriam and Aaron spake against Moses because of the
Ethiopian woman whom he had married: for he had married an
Ethiopian woman." (*Numbers* 12:1)

The Sorcerer Twardowski to His Spider

Now night is risen. One by one, the stars
like blossoms open. The tide is at its ebb.
Black seas draw back their cloaks to bare black bars
of blacker sand. The diamond hides its gleam.
'Tis time, Pajaku—wake within your web
between the moon's two ivory horns strung taut.
Descend upon the sleeping earth like Dream.
Drop down, through leagues of night, on silver
    thread
spun from the tails of comets you have caught
to steal, from perched atop each sleeper's head,
their restless words: each vow, each secret fear,
their songs, their choices, words of woe and cheer,
then whisper, little spider, in my ear,
for words are dear among the voiceless dead.

Pan Twardowski was a legendary Polish sorcerer who sold his soul
to the Devil and was stranded on the moon with his assistant, whom
he turned into a spider.

The Fairy Godmother to Cinderella

How *changed* you are! My magic didn't do it.
Some people shine as constant as the Dipper,
or simply shatter, easily as a slipper;
some shift from hard as glass to soft as suet.
Your clutch purse is again a day-old kipper,
your ruff once more a sheaf of autumn leaves,
your fan the bat that flaps about the eaves.
Oh, look!—your fan just ate your purse. That chipper
and *handsome* prince, who whirled you round the floor,
whose face was not too rough, but not too wan,
an eager raconteur, but not a bore,
who smiled so charming on the silk divan,
at midnight, or a little bit before,
can suddenly turn back into—a *man*.

Eudemus to Apollonius

I write this note in the sand because I know
the waves will wash it clean, and you won't see it.
Like the circles we traced here so long ago,
our footprints fade from Pergamum. So be it.
Your book was well received. As was your son;
his seems the echo of your dimming face.
How did my thoughts, which like an hourglass run,
once hold the eternal laws of boundless space?
The beach bends on forever. How might a man
reckon every mote, each grit and grain?
The universe of truths seems greater than
could ever fit within the human brain—
yet love, which binds over such a greater span,
is an infinite all mortals can contain.

---

150 BC. The first books of Apollonius of Perga's treatise on the
conic sections are dedicated to the geometer Eudemus of Pergamon.
Eudemus died before the fourth book was completed, and no other
information about him exists.

Artemisia to Pythius

The mouse, birthed from a mountain, finds an
    oyster
for its crypt. The Pharaohs build not tombs,
false mountains of rebirth. When Death's gate
    looms
the hermit sage is bricked within his cloister.
The arch of history bends not toward Justice
but to oblivion. In Hades' halls
what once were emperors' bones now deathless
    dust is;
their mortar-fied remains plug crumbling walls.
The winter's flaw is faltering by spring.
What vanity to think that I could bind
ourselves and immortality, could fling
a bottled torch into the dark behind—
just move these stones, and, like an Orphic song. . . .
Our shadows shall survive us. Not by long.

---

353 BC. Queen Artemisia of Caria built the Great Mausoleum, of
which Pythius was the architect.

Sophonisba to Gaia

How fickle our allegiances! How feigned
our feints and fancies. Why am I at fault
when Syphax couldn't snivel and exalt
the Glory That Is Rome and not sound pained?
My final freedom cannot be constrained;
I'll cruise the crystal spheres of Heaven's vault
while widow Dido's kingdom's sown with salt.
What form would Earth appear, this perch
    attained?
A sailor's map, faint shapes of seas and shores?
A Roman triumph, empty in its heart?
A nameless fray, no sanity, no start?
Unlabeled land, with life in every part?
And, as my shade through seas of starlight soars,
could I tell the earth the Romans rule from yours?

---

   203 BC. Sophonisba was a Carthaginian noble who drank
poison rather than be humiliated in a Roman victory parade.

The Nautilus-Shell Goblet to Holofernes

A pearl, dissolved in vinegar—or poison
in a cup that's crafted from a skull—
a gilt and porphyry vase to keep your toys in—
an urn filled with the world's ills, or full
of emperor's ashes—sweet Maronian wine—
a coupe of queen's champagne, bright, gold, and
    clear—
the cup that caught the Savior's blood—a stein
of milk and honey, when you wanted beer—
a bottle (beerless) tossed from wave to wave
until it found its—port—a butt of hock—
the final draught, poured out upon the grave—
the glass that holds in Time, drip-tick, drip-tock—
this drink is Death, and it will be your last.
Drink, General, I know you know the taste.

In the Book of Judith, the Assyrian general Holofernes is killed
after Judith gets him drunk at his own banquet.

Death to Donne

I have not pride. I have no vice! Which sin
could I commit? Would you suggest I lust?
Your flesh is putrid—presently, but dust.
Do I wax wroth? This face can't help but grin.
No shepherd ever slew so many sheep
as I my flock: does that make me a glutton?
Well, peek beneath this robe—I'm *rather* thin
(I must confess, I've never cared for mutton).
Perhaps it's sloth? I have been called "like sleep"
(in fact, we're twins). But day and night are twins
(my mother and my aunt). And I contend
that greed and envy, though two top-rate sins,
are concepts that I cannot comprehend—
how could I? See, it's *all* mine, in the end.

1631. After John Donne's "Holy Sonnet X."

Acknowledgments

Grateful acknowledgment is made to the editors of the following publications in which these poems, or earlier versions, first appeared:

Able Muse: "Casey to His Bat" and "Penelope to the Shuttle of Her Loom"

The Agonist: "Tinthu to Tesana"

Arion: "Emperor Tiberius to an Attendant," "Eudemus to Apollonius," "Glaucus to Anthedon," and "Thales to Thratta"

Ars Medica: "Semmelweis to Szent Rókus"

Atlanta Review: "Rhinthon to a Stranger at His Grave"

Better than Starbucks: "Theosebeia to Zosimos"

The Christian Century: "A Carpenter to a Carpenter"

Copperfield Review: "Dagobert to Childebert"

Extreme Sonnets II: "Miriam to Adoniah" and "Portrait"

First Things: "The Cat Jeoffry on Smart"

Gingerbread House: "The Fairy Godmother to Cinderella"

IthacaLit: "Cassandra to a Pithos in the Palace of the Pelopidae"

J Journal: New Writing on Justice: "Lucius Calpurnius Piso to Gnaeus Calpurnius Piso"

Jersey Devil Press: "The Lady of the House"

Journal of Humanistic Mathematics: "One Straight Line to Another Traveling in the Same Direction on an Infinite Plane"

Light: "George Auriol to a Patron at Le Chat Noir"

Lowestoft Chronicle: "Abaris to His Arrow"

The Lyric: "Ake to the Sea," "Alcibiades to a Mutilated Herm," "Crowhurst to the Sea," "Rosamund to the Skull of Cunimund," and "The Sorcerer Twardowski to His Spider"

Measure: "Andolosia to Ampedo," "The Great Poet," and "Mithridates to a Bee"

Modern Age: "A Monk of Newstead Abbey to Lord Byron" and "A Snowflake to Franz Wickmayer"

Montréal Writes: "The Ghost of Antigonish, Novia Scotia, to William Hughes Mearns" and "Soliloquy for an Imaginary Tragedy"

North American Anglican: "Suger to His Eagle"

Philosophy Now: "Proverbs for Engraving onto Imperial Monuments" and "Taurek to the Drowned Man"

Scrivener Creative Review: "Till to Pound"

Sein und Werden: "Artemisia to Pythius"

Snakeskin Poetry: "Antoine Simon to Louis-Charles Capet," "Arius Didymus to Octavian," "Baroness d'Olisva to a Queen of Diamonds," "Charles-Henri Sanson to His Son," "Fortunato to His Fetters," "Lucrezia to Lucretia," "The Nautilus-Shell Goblet to Holofernes," and "The Taco Bell Egg Taco to the Taco Bell Chicken Chalupa"

Society of Classical Poets Journal: "Gillette to Frenhofer," "Henrique to Malacca," "Pisanello to Serafina," and "Zaleucus to His Sword"

St. Austin Review: "Athanasius of Alexandria to a Satellite of Julian," "The Quadrifrons of Malborghetto to Constantino Pietrasanta," and "Young Augustine to a Pig"

THINK: "Nossis to a Traveler" and "A Salmon to the Sea"

Volare: "Pandora to Pyrrha"

Additionally, some of the poems in this collection are based on or adapted from other poems which first appeared in the following publications: the *Agonist*, the *Asses of Parnassus, Bad Lilies, Child of Words Fantasy & Science Fiction, Light, Lighten Up Online*, and the *Raintown Review*. This collection was a finalist for the 2021 Richard Wilbur Book Award.

Many of these poems I wrote while an undergraduate student at McGill University, about figures I studied in history, philosophy, and literature classes there. For this reason (and many others) I am indebted to my professors William Gladhill, Erica Harris, Iwao Hirose, Alison Laywine, Eric Lewis, and Oran Magal.

My parents, Beth Weinhouse and David Galef, provided invaluable feedback on many of the poems while they were being written and assembled. Their love and support is also pretty great to have, I guess.

I am extremely grateful to the editor of this volume, Alex Pepple, who has devoted countless hours to making this collection exist in the world.

And most of all this book would not exist without Eugene Lee-Hamilton, whose own poems were its inspiration.

Daniel Galef was born and raised in Oxford, Mississippi, where he spent his afternoons on the veranda of Square Books. After studying philosophy and classics at McGill University in Montreal, he received his MFA from the fiction program at Florida State University  in Tallahassee. His poetry covers a diverse range of styles and genres, including light verse (*Light Quarterly*, the *Saturday Evening Post*, the *Washington Post Style Invitational*), children's literature (*Spider*, the *Caterpillar*, *School Magazine*), and serious formal poetry (*Able Muse*, *Atlanta Review*, the *Lyric*). Besides poems, he also writes fiction (*Indiana Review*, *Juked*, the *Best Small Fictions* anthology), nonfiction (*Word Ways*, *Working Classicists*, the *Journal of Compressed Creative Arts*), humor and satire (*American Bystander*, *NationalLampoon.com*, the *Journal of Irreproducible Results*), and plays (Players' Theatre Montréal, Théâtre MainLine Theatre). In 2022 he placed second in the *New Yorker* cartoon caption contest. This is his first book.

ALSO FROM WORD GALAXY PRESS

David Alpaugh, *Spooky Action at a Distance – Poems*;
Seeing the There There – Poems

Barbara Lydecker Crane, *You Will Remember Me – Poems*

Daniel Galef, *Imaginary Sonnets – Poems*

Margaret Rockwell Finch, *Crone's Wines – Late Poems*

Emily Grosholz, *The Stars of Earth – New and Selected Poems*;
Traveling, Light and Dark, Discovery and Translation – Essays

A. G. Harmon, *Some Bore Gifts – Stories*

Elizabyth A. Hiscox, *Reassurance in Negative Space – Poems*

Sydney Lea and James Kochalka,
The Exquisite Triumph of Wormboy – Poems and Illustrations

Chukwuma Ndulue, *Holding Rain – Poems*

www.wordgalaxy.com

CPSIA information can be obtained
at www.ICGtesting.com
Printed in the USA
JSHW021124140323
38902JS00002B/174